Cottagecore

Things To Color, Cut Out, Paste & Collage

na hEireann Publishing 2021

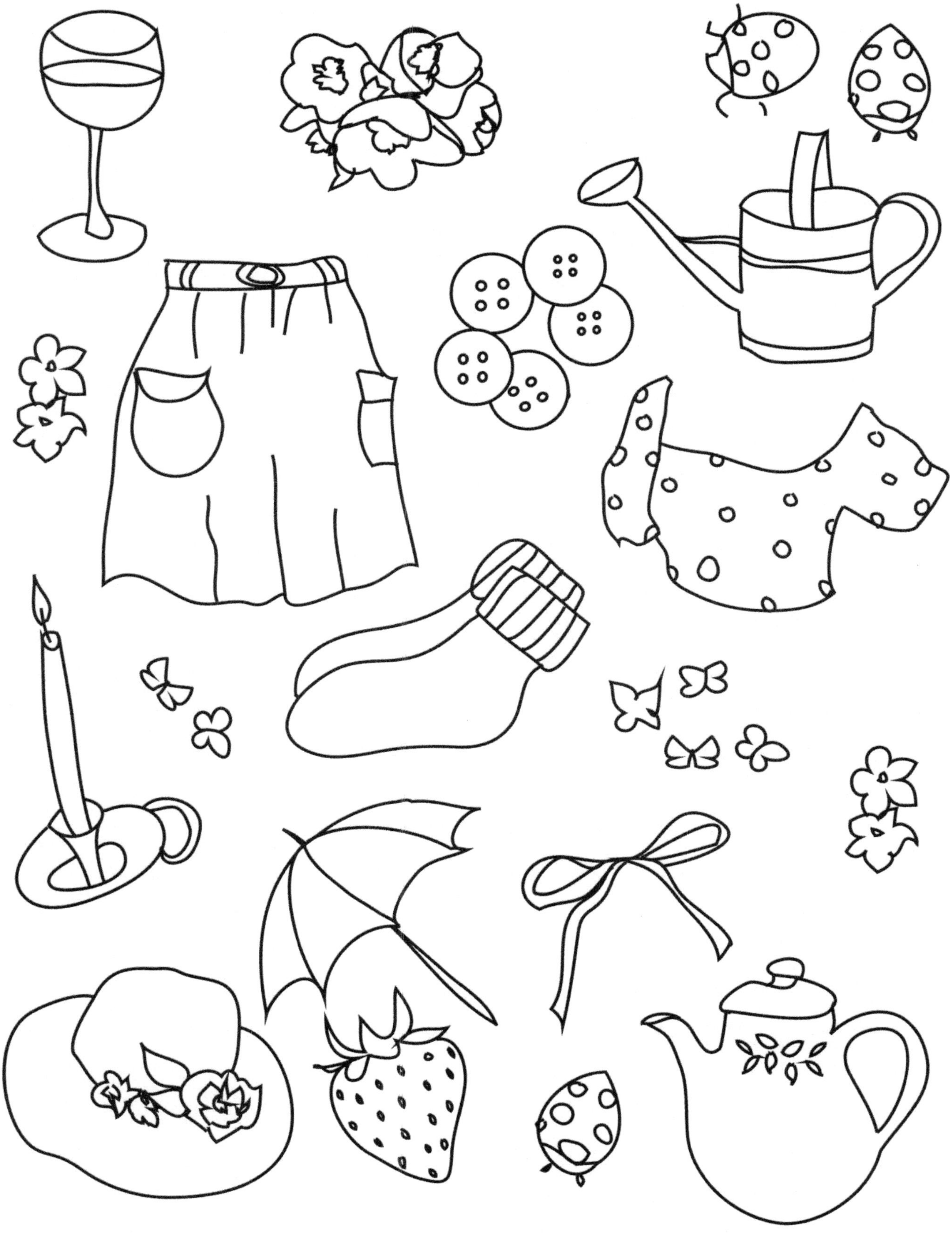

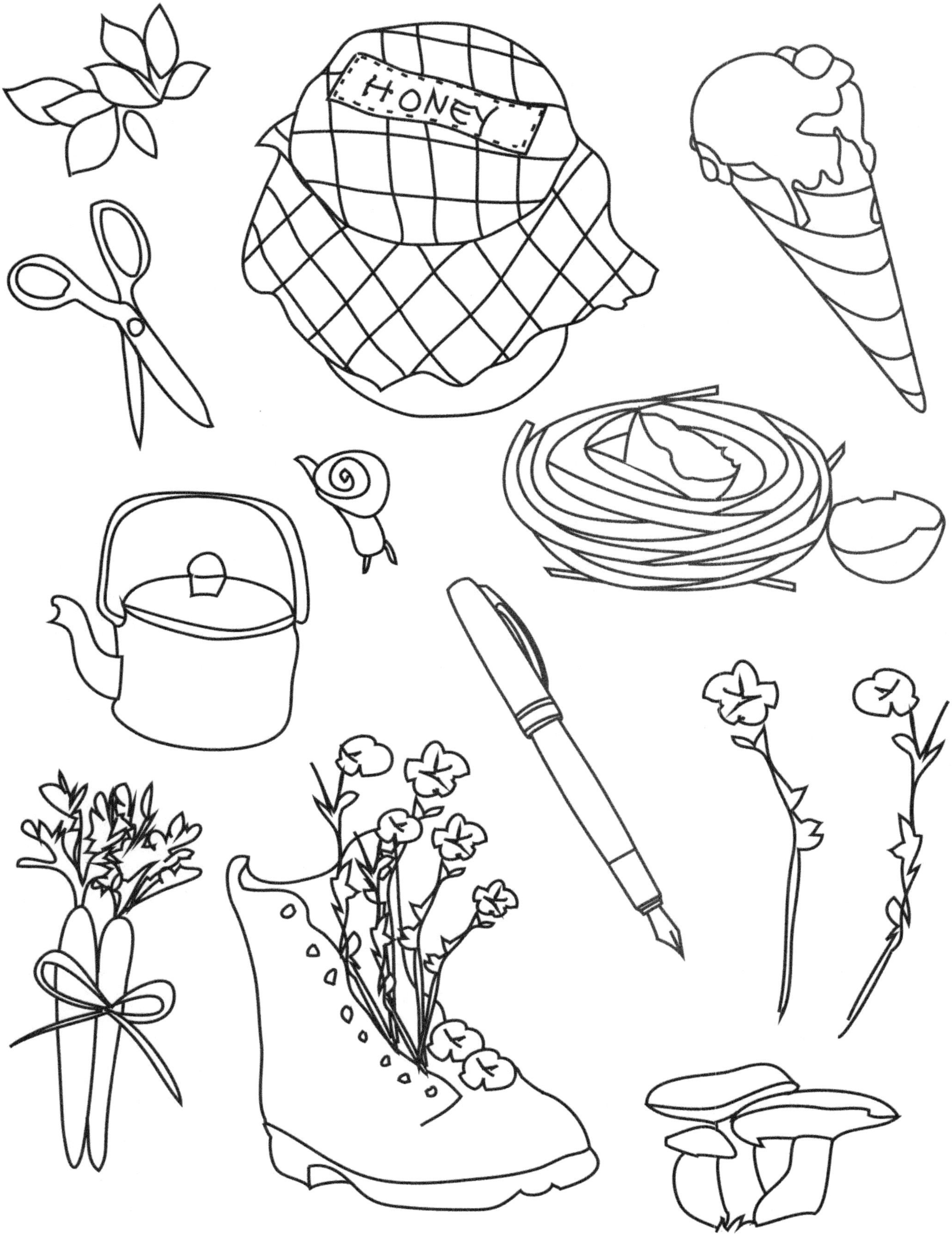
HONEY

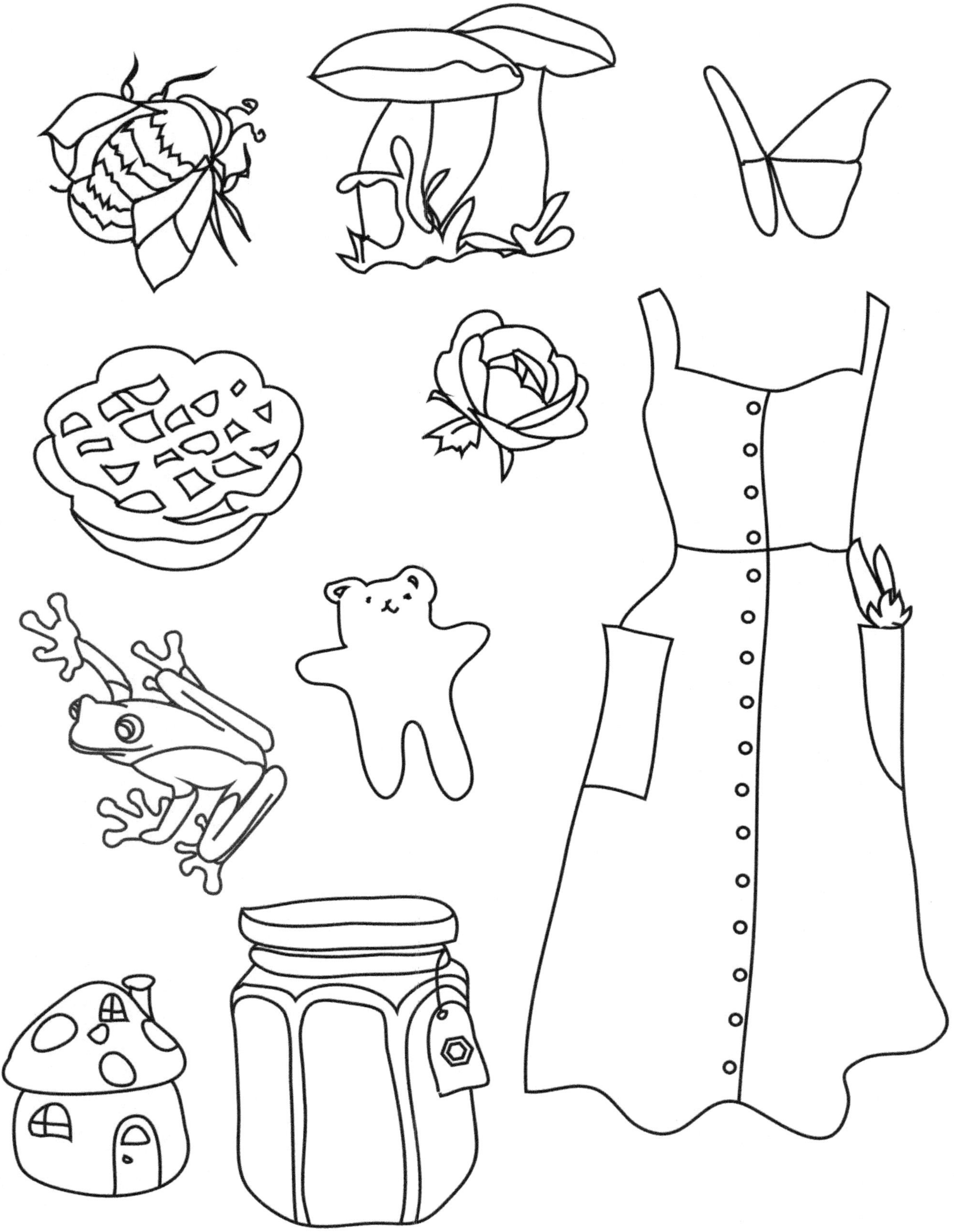

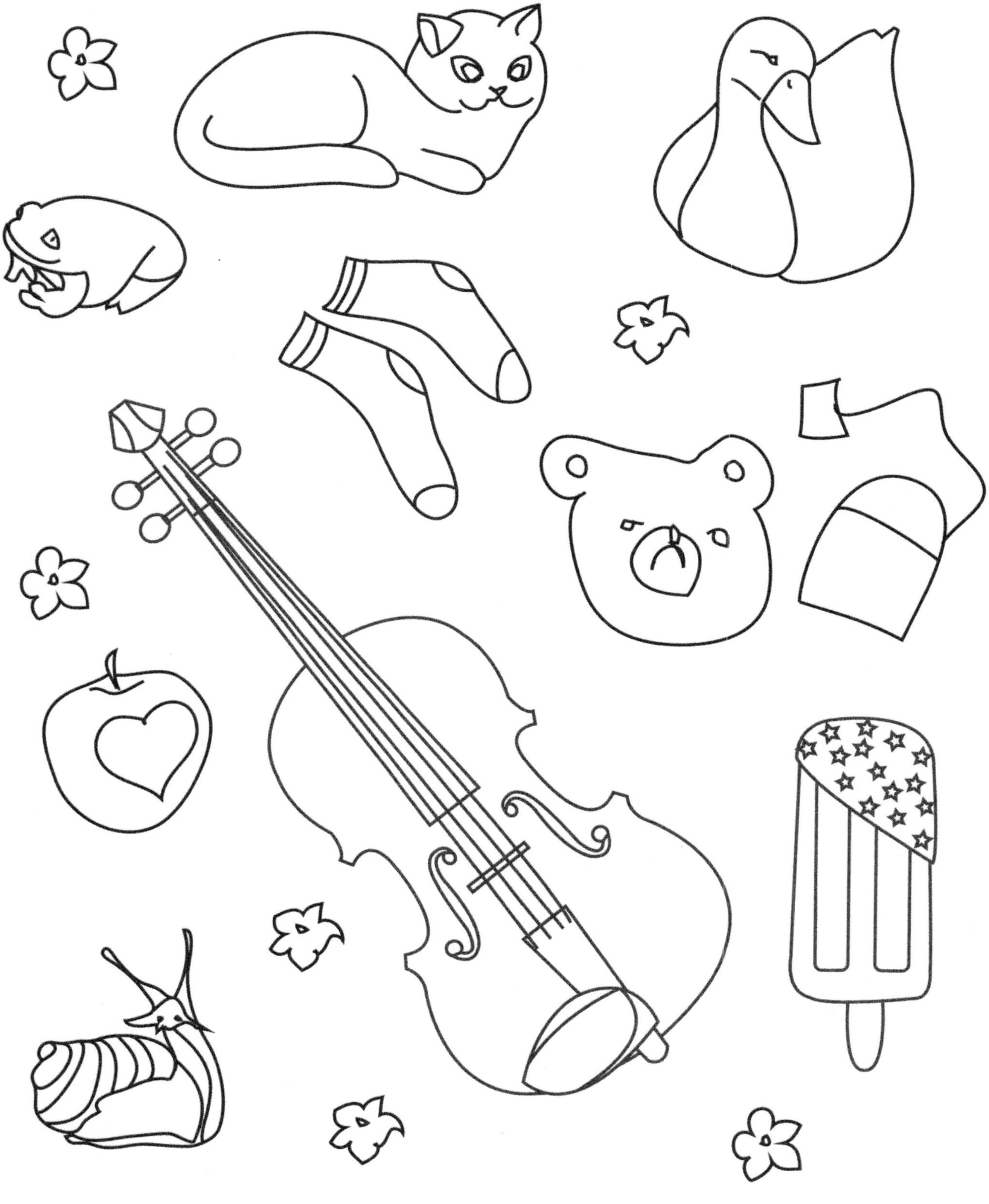

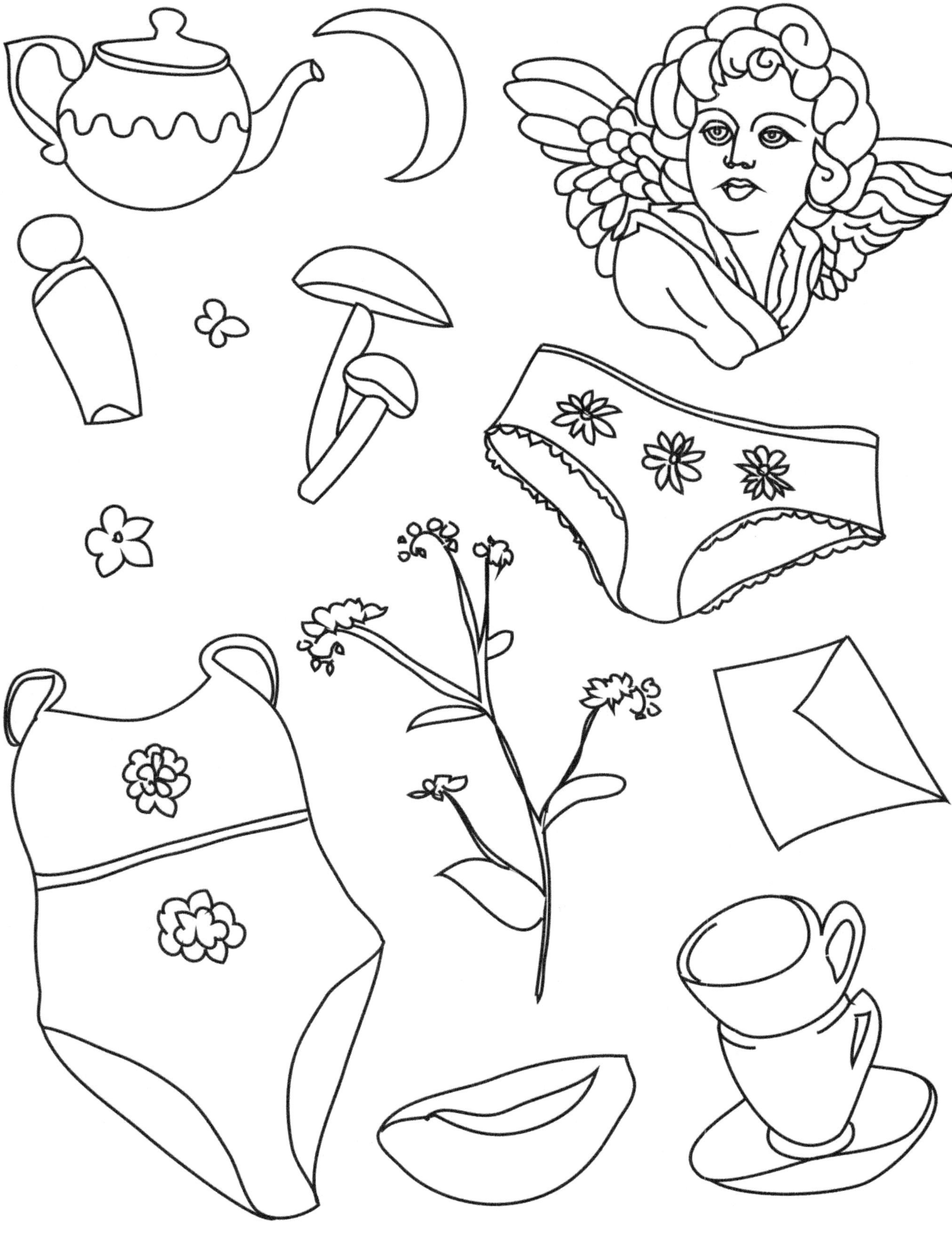

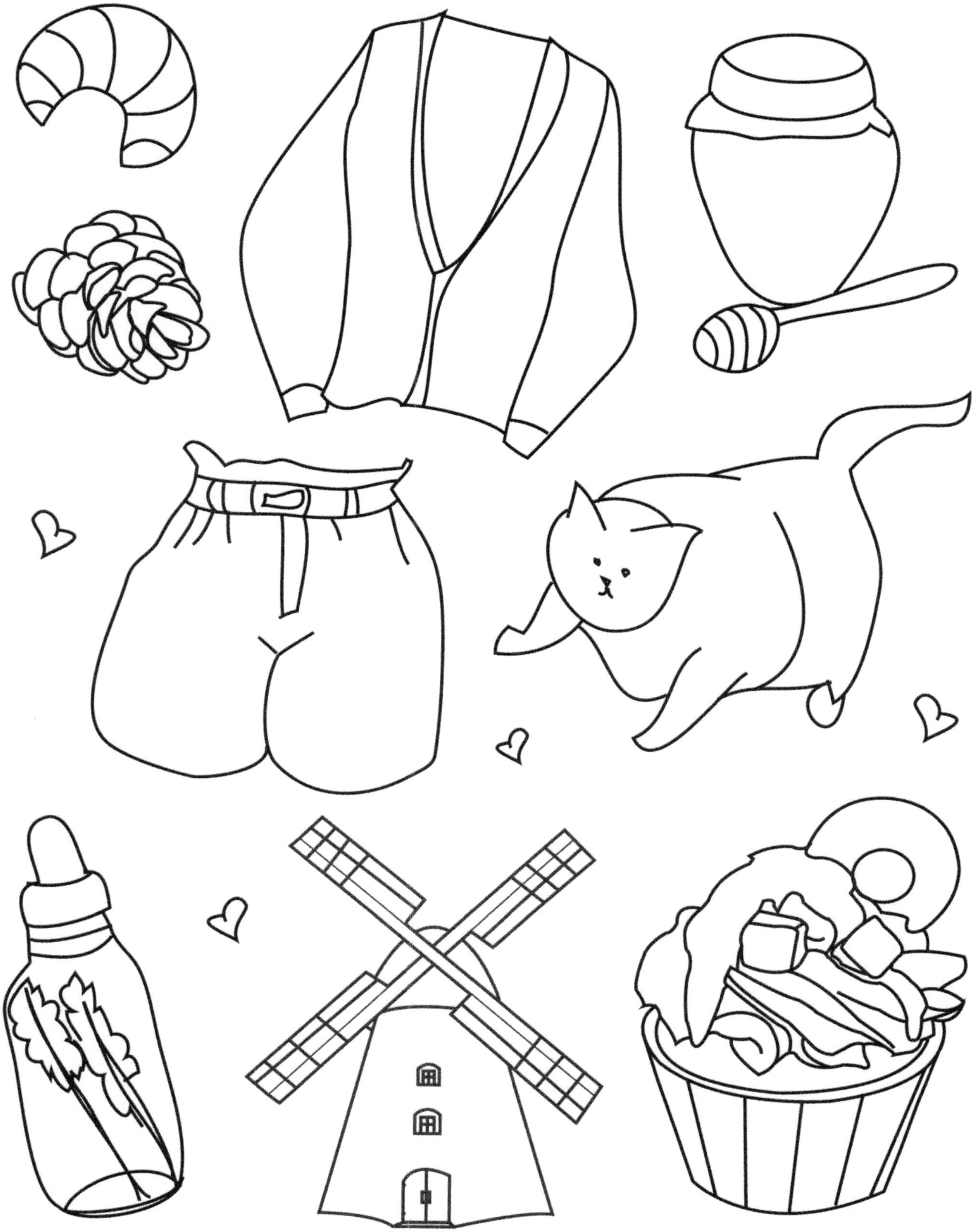

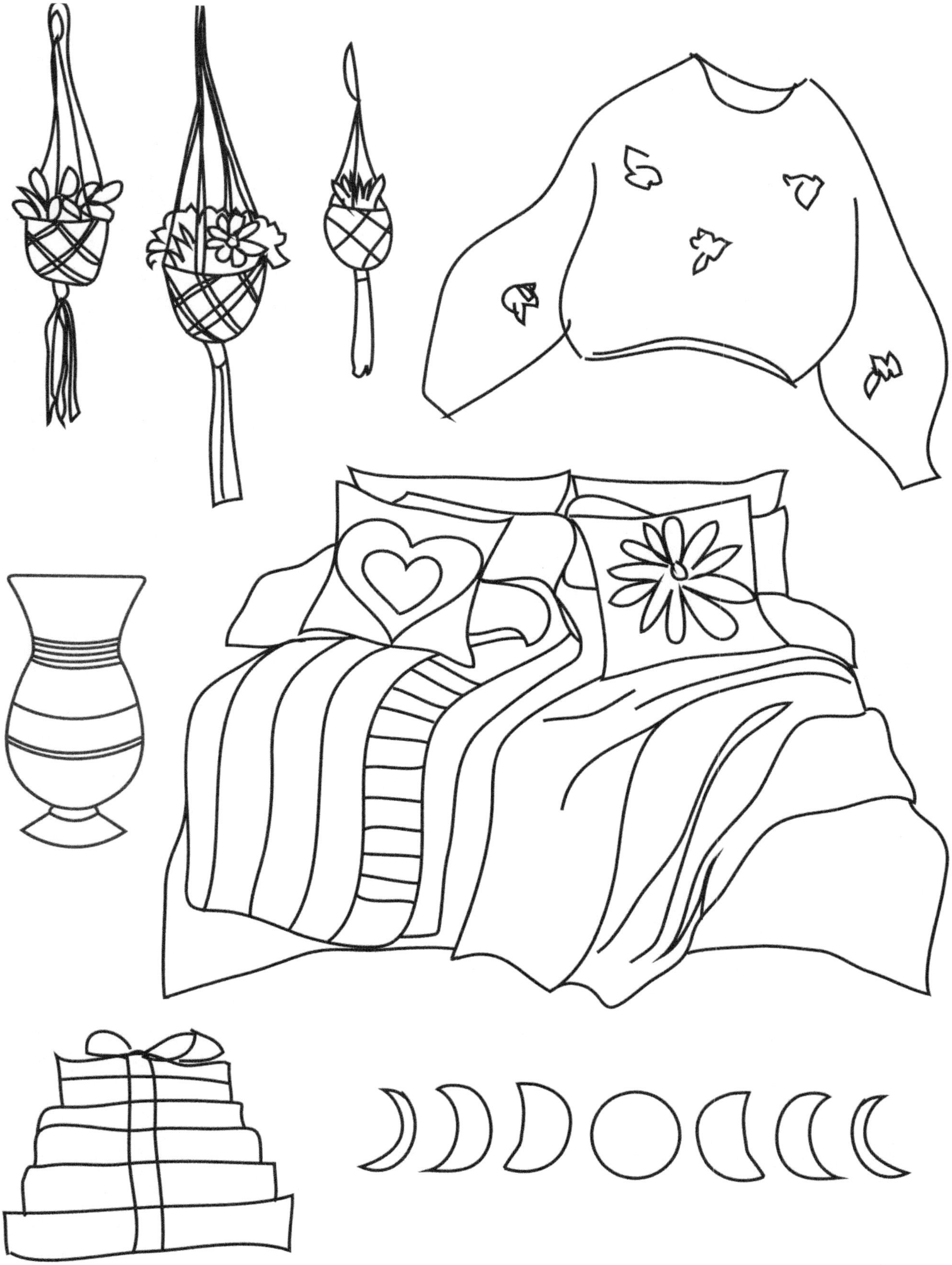

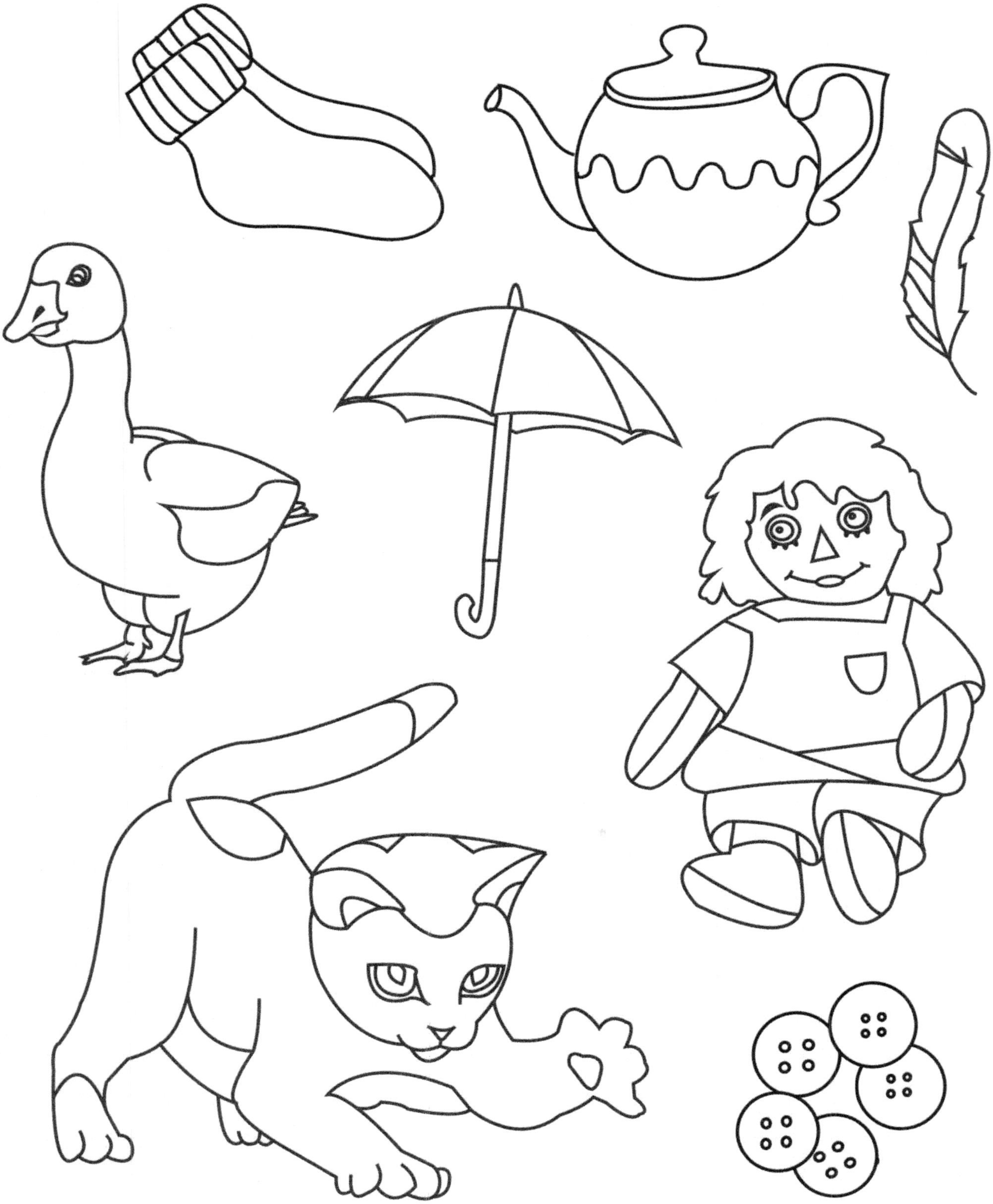

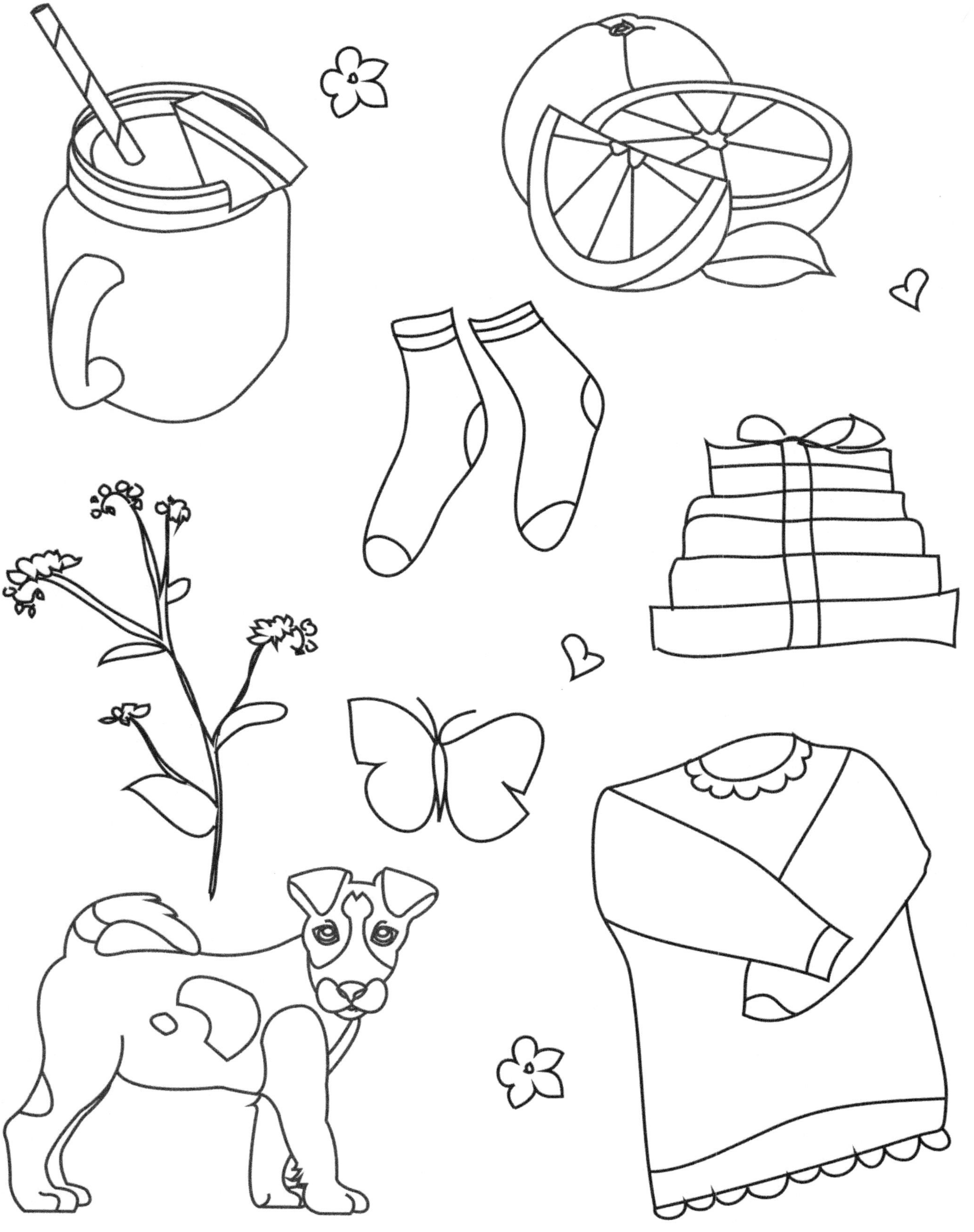

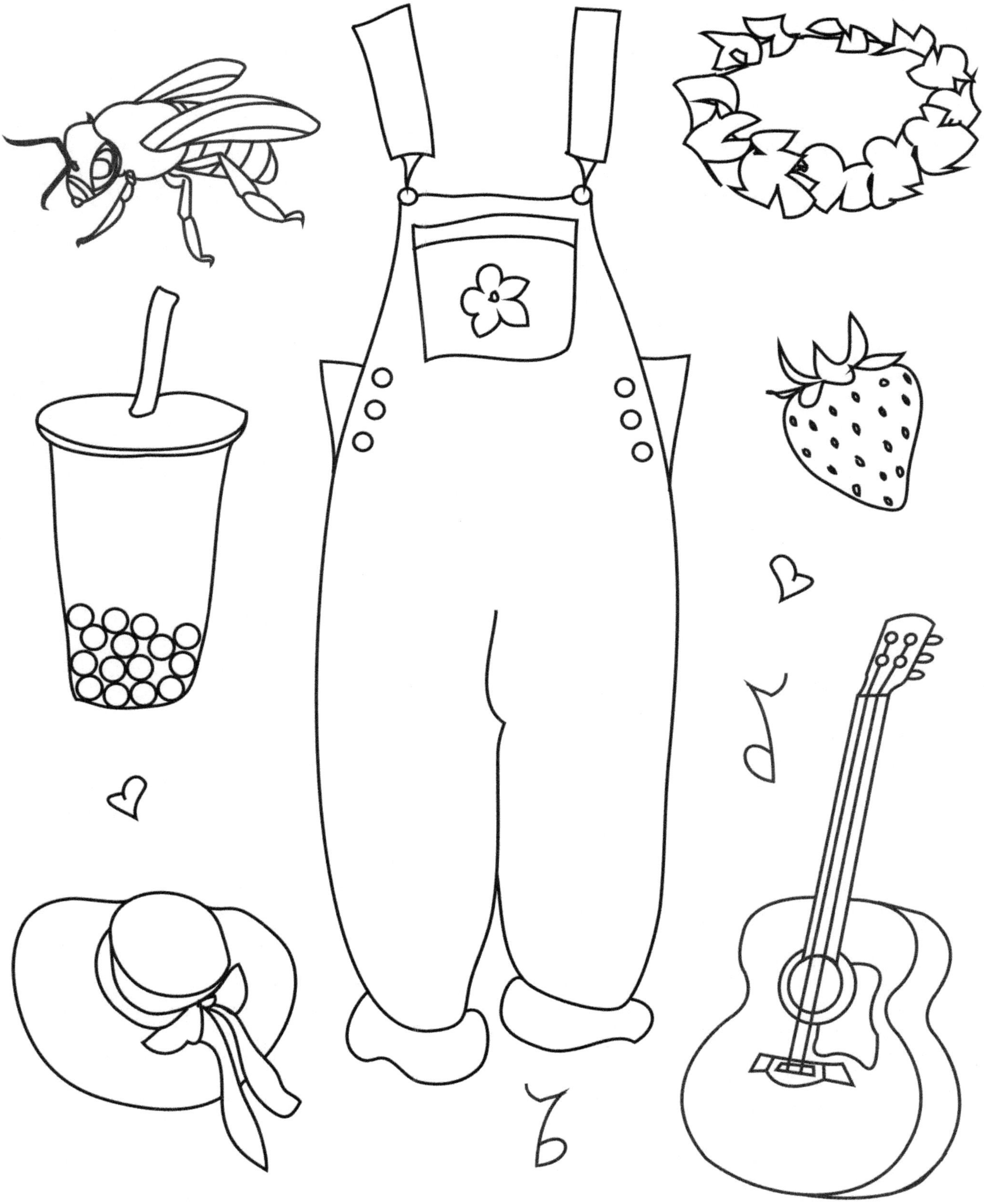

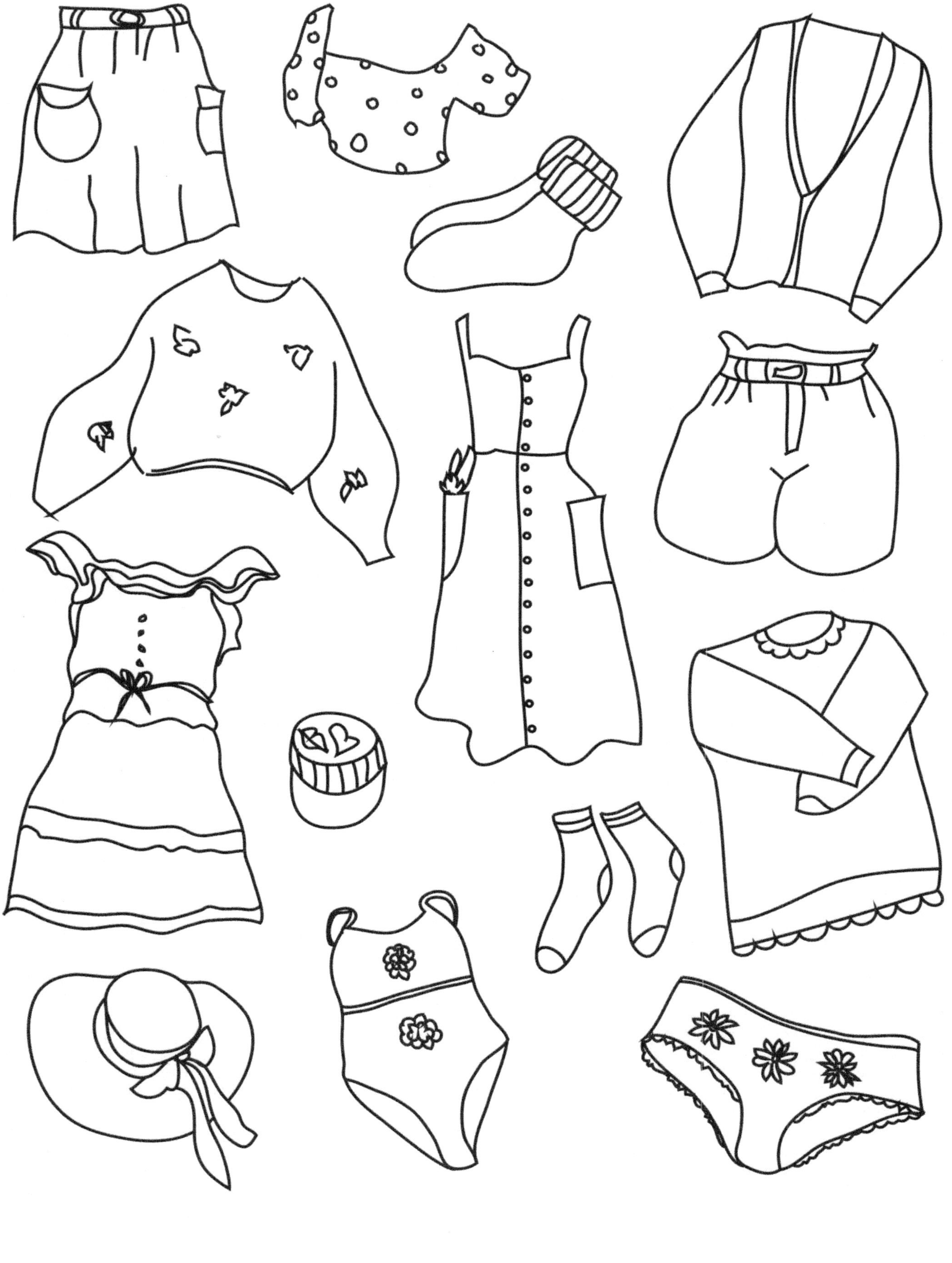

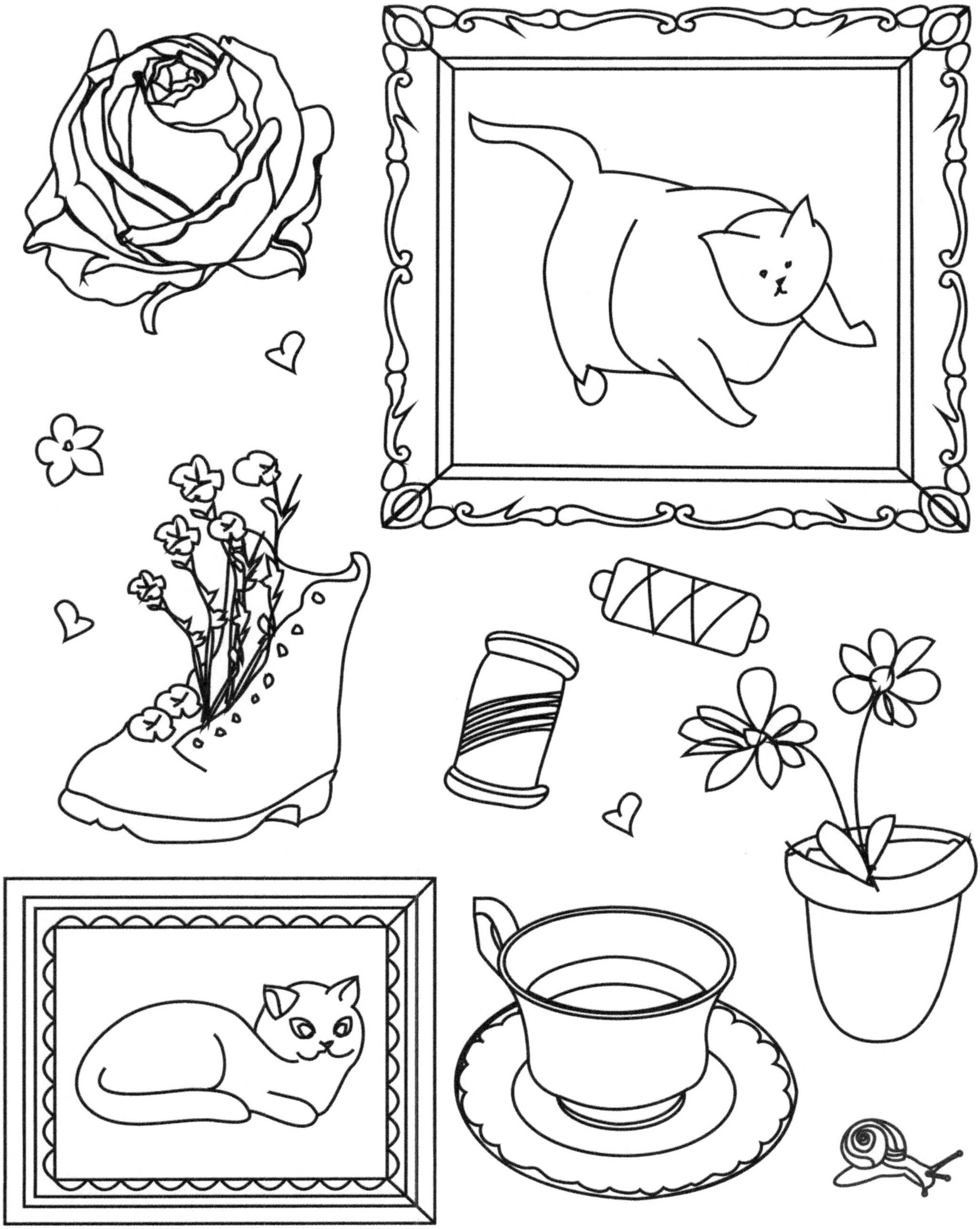

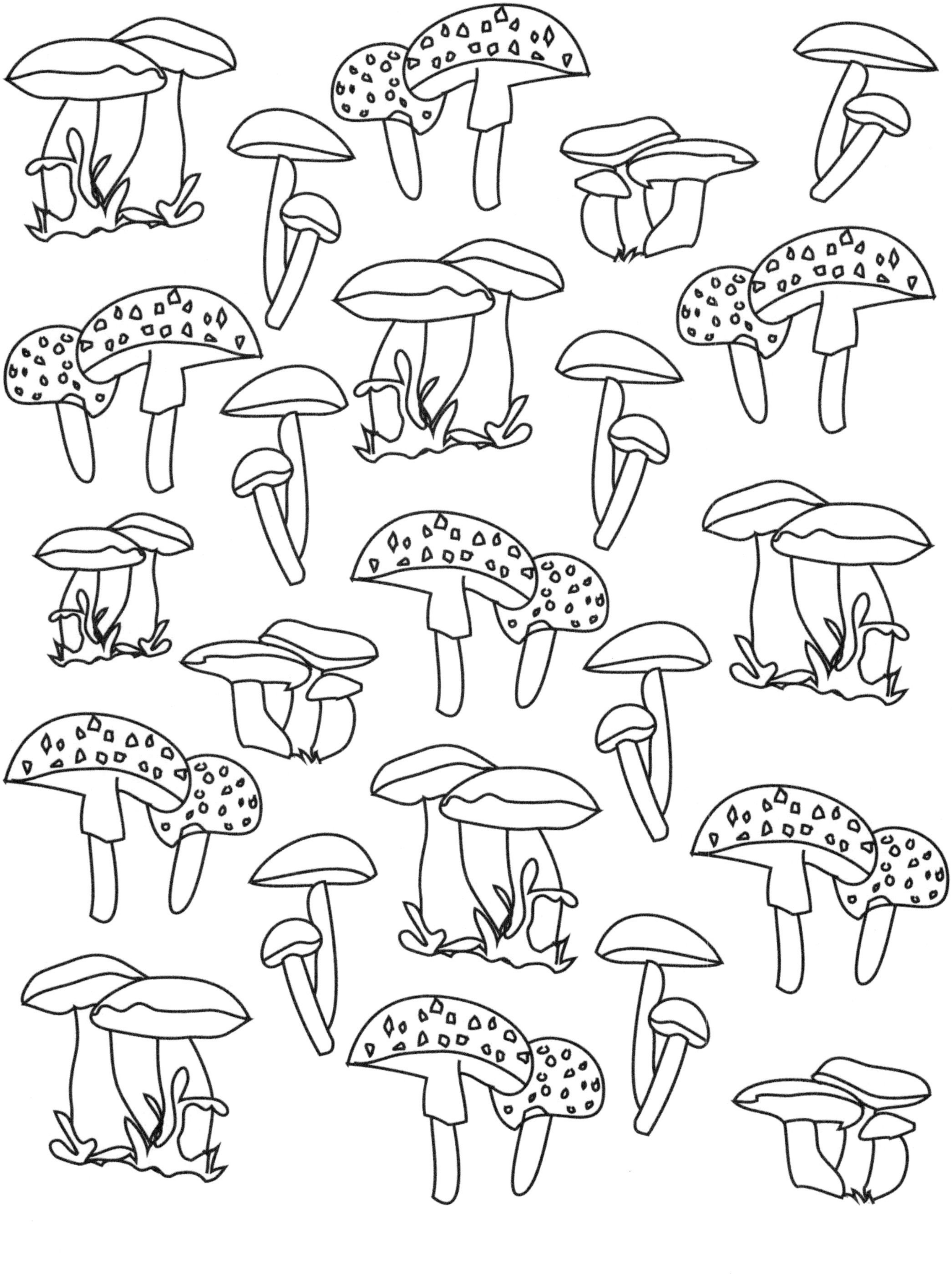

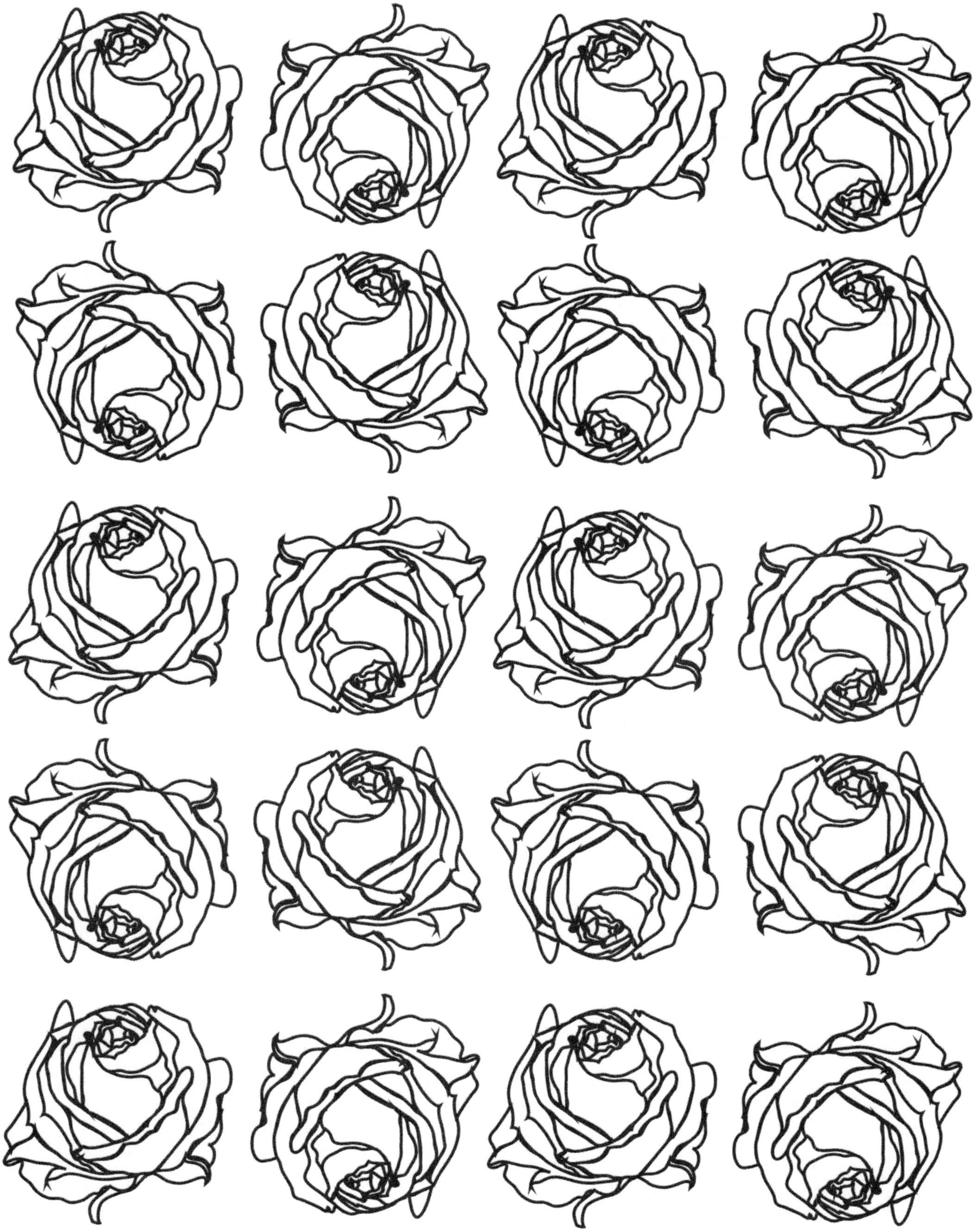

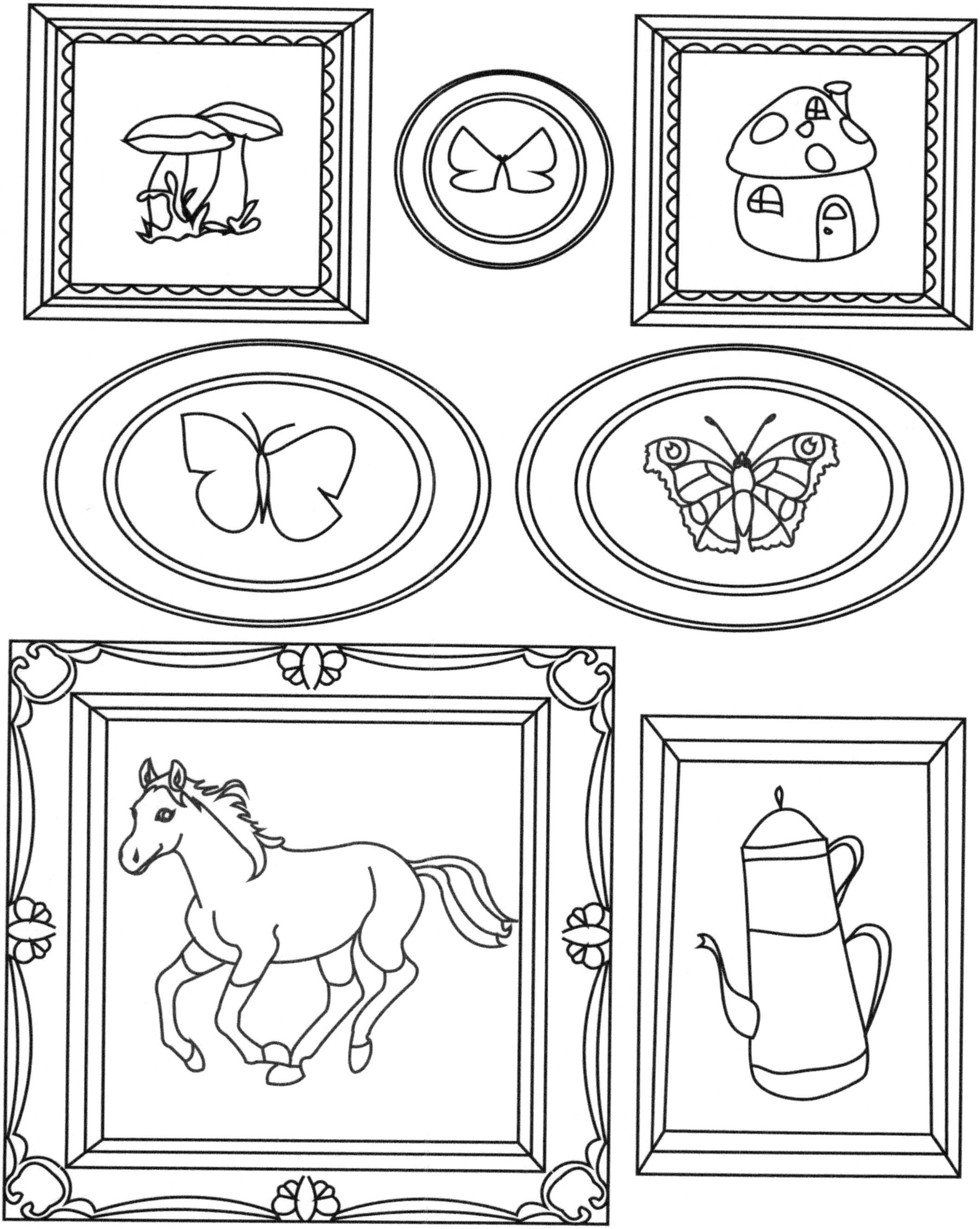

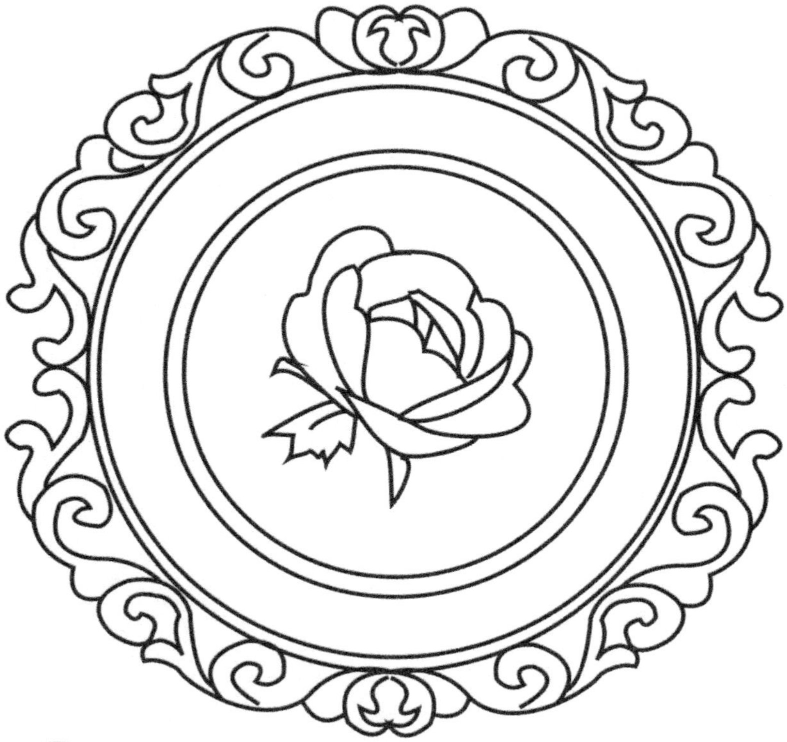
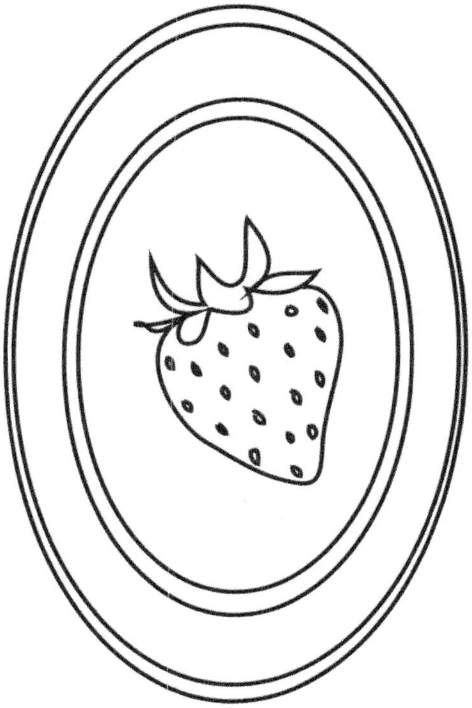
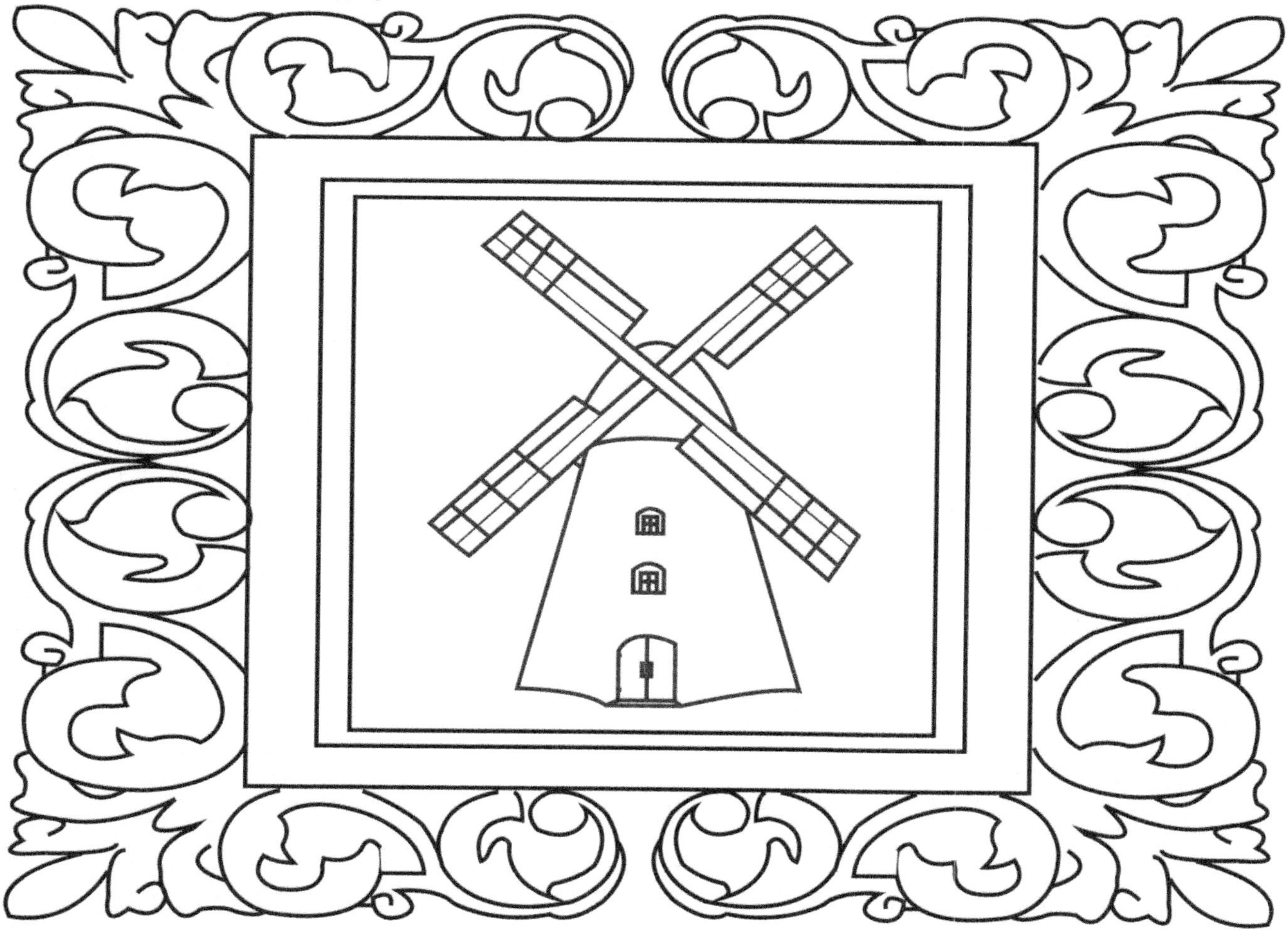

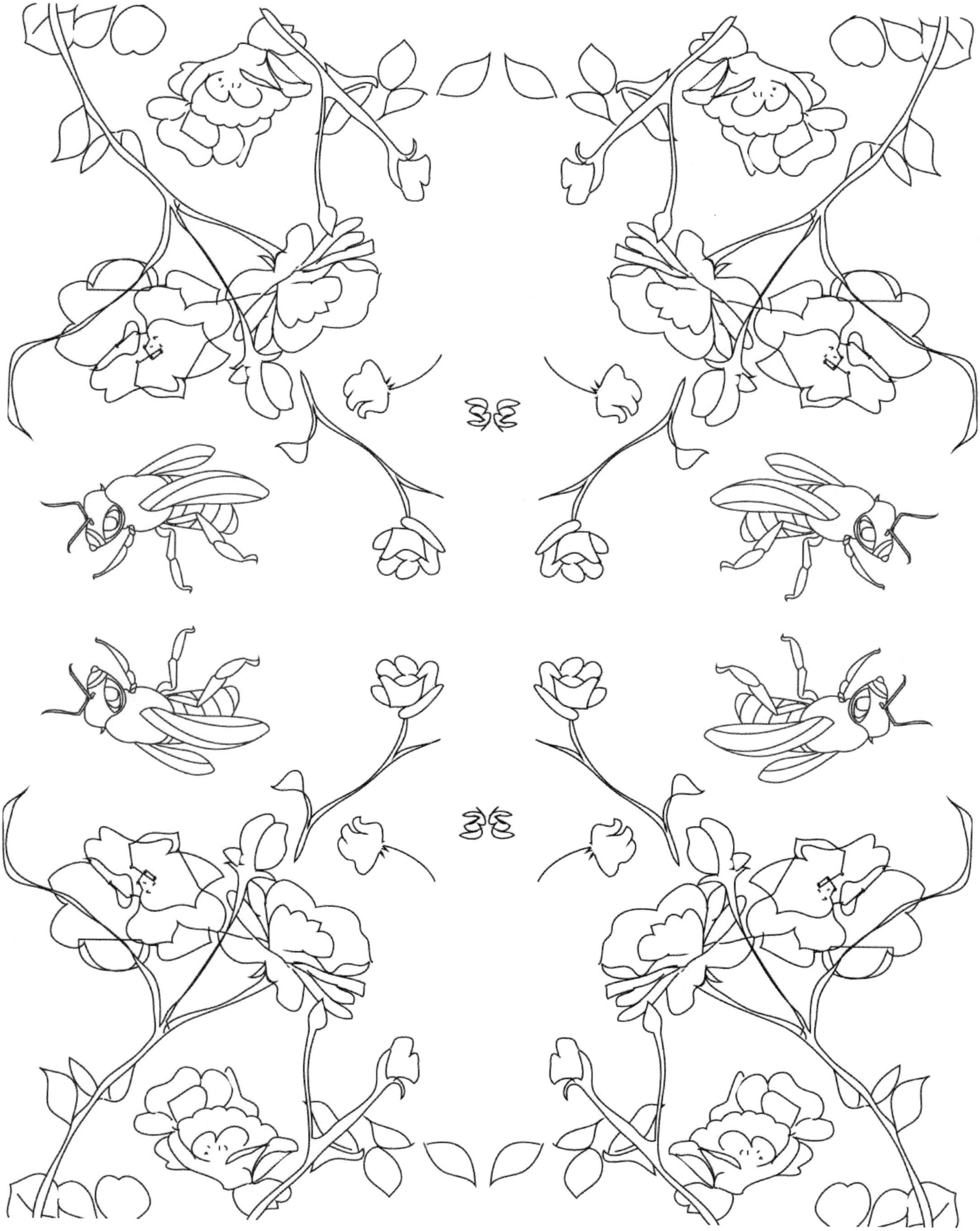

Printed in Great Britain
by Amazon

71705348R00025